ENGLISH TEATIME TREATS 2

THE BEST RECIPES FROM AROUND ENGLAND MADE SIMPLE

SANDRA HAWKINS

Second edition

Published by Great British Book Publishing, London

Great
British
Book
Publishing

ISBN: 978-0-9957623-2-9
ISBN: 978-0-9957623-3-6

DEDICATION

To Simon, Poppy, Monty and Barty - my inspirations!

"Taste and see that the Lord is good"

TABLE OF CONTENTS

INVITATION

You are cordially invited to join us to become a taster of the best recipes from around England made simple!

Sign up at the website below and you'll receive a FREE bonus recipe!

Check out the website for up-to-date promotions, competitions, the release date of future books, and all the latest news!

ett2.englishteatimetreats.com

INTRODUCTION

"I would love to make a teatime treat, but I certainly don't want the cleaning up afterward!"

"I think that baking is time-consuming and complicated - where are the simple, straightforward recipes which give fantastic results?"

"I seem to be stuck in a rut with buying the same treats or making the usual recipes, which are fine, but I'm rather bored with them. I would love to go to England and travel and taste the local treats!"

If any of these sound familiar, then this book is for you!

The English teatime treat recipes in this book are simple and need very little cleaning up afterward!

I guarantee:

- No electric mixers or food gadgets

- Very little rubbing in or rolling out

- No pile of cleaning up, and

- You don't need any special training or experience to make these recipes.

I can also guarantee that you will be enchanted by the stories that go with each recipe from Richmond Maids of Honor influenced by Henry VIII's wandering eye, Bosworth Jumbles, where the recipe was ripped from the dead hand of Richard III's cook on the battlefield, and Liverpool Tart which was originally created to help sailors avoid scurvy at sea.

Join me around England, stopping off at various places to taste the best recipes from those regions. I've included stories from each location, along with some fun facts about the recipe and ingredients, as well as a photograph of the baked treat.

I have been baking teatime treats since childhood. As I said in my first book, English Teatime Treats: Delicious Traditional Recipes Made Simple, I was taught to cook by my mother, grandmothers, great aunts, and by my Food and Nutrition teacher Mrs. Potts. Continuing my experimentation with cooking, I have completed a baking course on specialty cakes in London.

Having studied Chemistry at college, I have used my knowledge of the amazing processes that transform simple ingredients into mouth-watering treats to enhance and simplify traditional recipes. I have scoured the English countryside to bring you the best recipes from each area.

By creating something from scratch, you are seizing an opportunity to transform something mundane into a moment, a quick catch-up into a memorable occasion. Life is so busy and is remembered in these moments.

You are giving your precious time to friends and family, but only you will know that it didn't take long at all! And when you serve up the treat, you will be able to enhance the experience with a little piece of fun history or an amusing anecdote! Nothing draws people together like the warmth of a home-baked treat, the love that shows, and the laughter that accompanies it.

Be amazed by the variety of delicious traditional recipes, enjoy this virtual journey around England with me, and be enchanted by the wonderful stories.

Some recipes use pastry in a tart or pie. "But that's not simple!" I hear you cry! But you don't have to make the pastry; why not use a pre-baked pastry case and make only the filling! Or use a block of ready-made pastry, a packet-mix, or even ready-rolled pastry. What great chef doesn't have a sous-chef to help with the more basic and time-consuming tasks?

These versatile recipes can be used with pre-baked pastry cases, ready-made pastry, as well as your own. If you want to make your pastry, I have included a step-by-step guide as an Appendix - Pastry Tips to show you how.

Having been baking all my life, I have seen countless times that nothing makes people feel loved as a little dose of home baking.

English teatime treats lead the world in delicious home-baked treats. I can guarantee that you will be delighted with these recipes. There is nothing needlessly flashy about them, just delicious and wholesomely good.

This beautiful island nation has a rich and incredible history and has welcomed the influences of many cultures to our shores. This cultural diversity can be found in many of our recipes. You will be out of the rut of buying the same things and into a wide and wondrous exploration of tastes! You will discover hidden gems that I can guarantee will become firm family favorites.

Don't wait for inspiration to get baking; come on the journey with me now! You are likely to have most of the ingredients already, but if not, put them on the shopping list and make this the start of your journey into the best recipes from around England. If you make one recipe a week, in about six months, you will have traveled the country with me and enjoyed a new, delicious recipe every week.

Why not introduce an English teatime treat into your family routine? Or start an English Teatime Treats Club and get together with a group of friends to take it in turns to make one recipe a week, and there's the excuse to meet up! A surprise Coventry Godcake, a Bakewell Tart, or a teatime square of bright pink Tottenham Cake. Sharing and celebrating with friends and family could not be easier or more fun.

We shall be traveling around England, starting in London and moving clockwise and returning to complete our journey in London.

The map gives you the journey at a glance.

So let's begin together in London, the capital city of England and the United Kingdom, and the birthplace of the delicious Richmond Maids of Honor.

1. RICHMOND MAIDS OF HONOR

INTRODUCTION

We begin our tour in London, the capital of England and the United Kingdom and its largest city. For at least 2,000 years, there has been a settlement in the area. The name Londinium, given to the first large settlement by the Romans in about AD 46, has its origins in the Celtic language.

London has a rich, fairytale history, and having lived there for several years, much of this history is revealed in the streets you walk on and the historic buildings.

Queen Elizabeth II has ruled longer than any other British monarch. One of her royal residences is in central London, Buckingham Palace. If the Queen is in residence, the Royal Standard flies from the flagpole at the Palace.

Our first recipe comes from a previous monarch, Henry VIII, who reigned from 1509-1547 AD. Queen Elizabeth II is directly related to his father, Henry VII.

FUN FACTS

Rumor has it that one day as King Henry VIII was strolling through the grounds of Hampton Court Palace in Richmond, he saw a group of Maids of Honor, one of whom was Anne Boleyn, later to become his second wife.

The Maids, attendants to Henry VIII's first wife, Catherine of Aragon, were eating tarts and offered one to the King. He was so delighted with the pastries that he asked their name. The tarts had none, so Henry called them Maids of Honor.

These tarts were an invention of the pastry cook to Catherine of Aragon, and the recipe was a closely guarded secret for over 200 years. But now you can make and enjoy them yourself!

There are many variations on this recipe. Some even use shortcrust pastry and flavor the tartlets with jam. But the most traditional use lemon curd, curd cheese, and puff pastry. They are very light and melt in the mouth.

INGREDIENTS

Makes 24

- 18 oz. (500g) block puff pastry (or pre-rolled)

- 1 cup (225g) cream cheese

- ¼ cup (40g) superfine (caster) sugar

- Zest 2 lemons

- ⅓ cup (30g) ground almonds

- 1 large egg plus 1 large egg yolk

- 4 tbsp. good-quality lemon curd

- Powdered (icing) sugar for dusting

- You will also need a 3¼ inch (8 cm) plain cutter and two 12-hole shallow muffin pans, greased.

METHOD

1. Preheat the oven to 400°F (200°C).

2. Cut the pastry block in half, roll out, and cut 12 circles from each half, or unroll your pre-rolled pastry and cut out 24 circles using a 3¼ inch (8 cm) plain cutter.

3. Line the tins with the pastry circles.

4. In a bowl, combine the cream cheese, sugar, lemon zest, ground almonds, then beat in the egg and egg yolk.

5. Mix thoroughly with a balloon whisk until everything is very evenly blended.

6. Spoon half a teaspoon of lemon curd into the base of each pastry case and then spoon a heaped teaspoon of the cream cheese mixture on top of this.

7.   Bake the tarts in the oven for about 20-25 minutes. The mixture will have puffed up and turned a light golden-brown color.

8.   Take them out of the oven and transfer them to a wire rack to cool. Don't worry if the tarts start to sink a little, that's absolutely normal!

I suggest giving them a faint dusting of icing sugar before you serve them.

After tasting the fare of Henry VIII's court, from Hampton Court Palace in Richmond, southwest London, we travel 16 miles to the East End of London and sample something called, intriguingly, London Stuffed Monkey Pie.

2. LONDON STUFFED MONKEY PIE

INTRODUCTION

From the 16th century court of Henry VIII, we travel forward several hundred years to 19th century East End London for a recipe that has its roots in the Jewish Community.

Between 1881 and 1914, more than 2 million Jews left Eastern Europe, prompted by economic hardship and increasingly ferocious persecution.

Many Jews landing in England intended to go to America, but about 120,000 remained in the UK. Large numbers found a home in Spitalfields, in the East End, and brought with them their culture and recipes.

FUN FACTS

Jewish bakeries and food sellers thrived in the East End of London, and this pie was one of the most beloved.

There are several possible explanations for the odd name "stuffed monkey pie." The "stuffed" part is self-explanatory as it refers to the fruit inside the pie.

The "Monkey" part could have come from the Arabic word for stuffed, "makhshi." It is also possible "Monkey" is a shortened version of the name of the Dutch Jewish family, Monnickendam, who made them. Either way, it is an unusual and delicious pie.

This pie uses mixed or candied peel, which is orange and lemon peel soaked in sugar to preserve the flavor. If you can't get this ingredient, substitute with other dried fruit and add the grated zest of a lemon and an orange to the filling.

INGREDIENTS

Serves 8

For the pastry base and lid

- 18 oz. (500g) shortcrust pastry, divided into two

For the filling

- 3 tbsp. (40g) butter
- ⅔ cup (100g) ground almonds
- 1 cup (100g) chopped mixed peel or candied peel
- ½ cup (60g) currants
- 1 egg yolk
- ½ tsp. vanilla extract
- 9" (23 cm) cake pan

For the topping

- 1 egg white
- 1 tbsp. superfine (caster) sugar
- 1 tbsp. sliced or flaked almonds

METHOD

1. Preheat the oven to 375°F (190°C) and place a baking sheet in there to heat.

2. Roll out half of the pastry and line the pie pan; no need to bake blind.

3. Melt the butter and stir in the ground almonds, chopped mixed peel, currants, egg yolk, and vanilla extract.

4. Spread the filling mixture over the pastry base.

5. Roll out the other half of the pastry and place the lid on the pie. Seal around the edges by pressing down.

6. Brush with egg white, sprinkle with sugar and sliced or flaked almonds.

7. Place the pie on the hot baking sheet in the oven and bake for about 25 minutes.

Serve warm or cold with cream or ice-cream.

We leave London and travel 41 miles southeast to the lovely county of Kent. The town of Maidstone is home to delicious rose-flavored buttery biscuits called Maidstone Biscuits.

3. MAIDSTONE BISCUITS

INTRODUCTION

Maidstone in Kent formally became a town when granted a royal charter in 1549 AD. It would regain and lose its title several more times over the centuries.

The name Maidstone is derived from the Saxon word meaning "the maidens' stone" and is mentioned in the Domesday book of 1086 AD. The settlement was noted for its salt production, eel fishing, and flour milling.

Interestingly, the local limestone, quarried from Roman times, was used at Hampton Court Palace and the Tower of London.

FUN FACTS

These biscuits are different from American biscuits, which are more scone-like. The International Dictionary of Food and Cooking describes these types of pastries as a light, crisp biscuit.

The use of rose water and almonds suggests that it comes from Medieval times when these ingredients were widely used in country manors.

It has a taste of early English summer about it, and you can almost feel the fresh warmth of the sun on your face.

INGREDIENTS

Makes about 28.

- 1 cup or 2 sticks (200g) butter, softened

- 1 cup (200g) superfine (caster) sugar

- 2½ cups (300g) all-purpose (plain) flour

- 4 tsp. rose water

- ⅔ cup (100g) blanched almonds, chopped

- 2 baking sheets lined with parchment paper

METHOD

1. Preheat the oven to 350°F (180°C).

2. Cream the butter and sugar together in a bowl until pale and fluffy. So long as the butter is soft, the creaming is easy.

3. Fold in the flour, rose water and blanched almonds, and mix to make a stiff dough. Bring the dough together with your hands.

4. Form walnut-sized balls and place them on the baking sheet. Squash each ball down a little with three fingers.

5. Bake for 12-15 minutes until golden brown.

6. Cool on a wire rack.

Traveling 28 miles due east brings us to Canterbury, where we will try the surprisingly creamy and tangy Canterbury Lemon and Apple Tart.

4. CANTERBURY LEMON AND APPLE TART

INTRODUCTION

The Cathedral enjoys over a million visitors a year and is well worth a visit. It has beautiful stained-glass windows, and it is a little eerie to stand on the altar steps where Thomas Becket, the Archbishop of Canterbury, met his Maker some 850 years ago.

The infamous murder of Thomas Becket took place on 29th December 1170 AD. There was indeed a battle for control of the church between Henry II and the Archbishop of Canterbury, Thomas Becket, which triggered Becket's murder in 1170 AD. Though I can't help but feel the actual murder of the Archbishop was based on a misunderstanding.

The story goes that Henry II was so frustrated with the Archbishop that he declared, "Will no one rid me of this troublesome priest?" This was more of an exasperated cry than a command. However, unfortunately, four knights overheard him and went to Canterbury to find Becket. These knights confronted and murdered Becket as he struggled on the steps of the altar inside Canterbury Cathedral. I guess one of the morals of this story is it's good to try to be careful what we say out loud!

FUN FACTS

Kent is known as the Garden of England because it boasts of so many plentiful orchards. Apples have been grown around the world, and the Romans created many new varieties. Pliny (first century AD) listed 22 types and described how farmers would auction the fruit from their trees.

The practice of auctioning fruit from trees continues to this day near Canterbury, in the county of Kent.

Canterbury Lemon and Apple Tart is a wonderfully lemony tart with a gooey center because of the grated apples.

INGREDIENTS

Serves 8

- 13.2 oz. (375g) shortcrust pastry to line 9 inch (23 cm) removable bottom cake pan or a pre-baked pastry case

- ½ cup or 1 stick (100g) butter, melted

- 4 eggs

- 1 cup (225g) superfine (caster) sugar

- 2 lemons, grated zest, and juice

- 2 large cooking apples (Bramley, or similar), quartered, cored and peeled

- 2 eating apples, cored and finely sliced, no need to peel (red ones look great unpeeled)

- 1 tbsp. (25g) Demerara sugar

METHOD

1. Preheat a baking sheet in the oven to 400°F (200°C).

2. Line the cake pan with pastry and put it in the fridge while you make the filling.

3. Melt the butter in a pan.

4. In a large mixing bowl, beat together the eggs, superfine (caster) sugar, lemon zest, and juice, and add the melted butter.

5. Grate the cooking apples straight into the bowl using a coarse grater and stir in.

6. Remove the cake pan from the fridge and pour the apple mixture into it, and then slice the eating apples and place artistically around the top.

7. Sprinkle the sugar all over the eating apples.

8. Bake on the preheated baking sheet for about 40 minutes. The tart needs to be set in the center, and slightly brown.

We now travel 58 miles southwest from Canterbury to the beautiful village of Ripe nestled on the Downs in East Sussex for our next recipe, Sussex Cherry Tart.

5. SUSSEX CHERRY TART

INTRODUCTION

The village of Ripe was owned by Earl Harold, later to become King Harold, who was killed at the Battle of Hastings in 1066 AD. Ripe lies north of the Downs, and these hills can be seen all around the village.

Sussex is home to Arundel Castle, very close to where we live. It is a magnificent castle, established on Christmas Day 1067 AD. It is open to the public but is also the home of the Duke of Norfolk and his family. A real treat is visiting in the summer when there is a Shakespeare play performed in the Earl's garden.

The Castle also has a beautiful cricket pitch with stunning views to the Downs, where we have enjoyed a few gentle afternoons. It is essential to bring a flask of tea and some Sussex Cherry Tart!

FUN FACTS

Cherries have been grown in the area for hundreds of years, and there is even a recipe for a cherry tart that dates to the time of Richard II in 1390 AD.

It has a frangipane middle made with ground almonds, which stays moist during cooking. The tart may have its roots in an annual local pie feast that celebrated the cherry harvest. Variations include substituting sliced apples or pears for the cherries.

INGREDIENTS

Serves 8

- 13.2 oz. (375g) shortcrust pastry to line 9 inch (23 cm) removable bottom cake pan or a pre-baked pastry case

- ⅓ cup (75g) butter, softened

- ½ cup (75g) ground almonds

- ⅓ cup (75g) superfine (caster) sugar

- 1 large egg

- 1½ cups (200g) cherries - frozen are fine

METHOD

1. Preheat the oven to 400°F (200°C) and place in a baking sheet to heat.

2. Line the cake pan with pastry and bake blind. (See Appendix - Pastry Tips for how to do this.) Or use a pre-baked pastry case.

3. Beat together the butter, ground almonds, sugar and egg.

4. Spread over the pastry case.

5. Drop the cherries into the almond mixture in a regular pattern. They should cover the almond mixture in one even layer. Push them in slightly.

6. Bake in the oven for 35-40 minutes.

Serve warm or cold with cream or ice-cream.

Traveling west some 175 miles brings us to the county town of Taunton in Somerset to taste the Somerset Apple Tart.

6. SOMERSET APPLE TART

INTRODUCTION

Somerset is so named by the ancient Welsh Celts and Saxons as they could only live off the land during the summer months.

Apples have been grown in England for millennia. There are so many apple orchards in Somerset that the local authority has a tree planting Project Officer who can offer free practical advice on planting orchards!

Somerset County Council was the first county to give grants for orchard conservation, and the Council has continued to try to keep orchards as part of the landscape and to find outlets for the fruit.

FUN FACTS

This particular tart looks beautiful with the arranged apple slices but also has a creamy sweetness to the custardy apple filling. It is a favorite of my husband's, as he grew up in Somerset.

The Bramley apple name comes from Matthew Bramley, who, in 1856, allowed a local nursery worker to take cuttings from the tree in his garden and to start selling the apples. The only condition was that the apples bore his name. Bramley apples are almost exclusively a British variety, so for the recipe, if you can't find them, just use a different sharp-tasting variety.

The Bramley apple is sour if eaten raw, but when cooked, it has a much more gentle flavor and is light and fluffy.

INGREDIENTS

Serves 8

- 13.2 oz. (375g) shortcrust pastry to line 9 inch (23 cm) removable bottom cake pan or a pre-baked pastry case

- 3 Bramley apples (or other sharp apples such as Granny Smiths)

- ½ cup (125 ml) single cream

- 1 large egg

- ¼ cup (50g) superfine (caster) sugar

- ½ tsp. vanilla extract

- 9" (23 cm) cake pan

METHOD

1. Preheat the oven to 350°F (180°C) and place in a baking sheet to heat.

2. Line the cake pan with pastry and bake blind. (See Appendix - Pastry Tips for how to do this.) Or use a pre-baked pastry case.

3. Peel and slice the Bramley apples and spread artistically over the pastry base.

4. Whisk together the cream, egg, sugar, and vanilla extract.

5. Pour over the apples and bake in the oven on the preheated baking sheet for 30-35 minutes.

Our next stop is the city of Exeter in the county of Devon, some 32 miles southwest.

Here we shall sample the traditional Devonshire Splits, made locally with fresh cream from the many dairy herds grazing on the hills.

7. DEVONSHIRE SPLITS

INTRODUCTION

We have nipped west over the county border from Somerset into Devon.

It is from this county that the biscuits were made that sustained the Pilgrim Fathers in 1620 AD when sailing on the Mayflower to the New World.

Exeter, in Devon, has the narrowest street in England, Parliament Street only 25 inches at its most tapered.

FUN FACTS

Have you ever wondered from where the tradition of eating bread, jam, and cream comes?

Historians in Tavistock, Devon, think they have found the answer.

They studied ancient manuscripts as part of the research leading up to the 900th anniversary of the granting of Tavistock's Royal Charter by King Henry I in 1105 AD. Tavistock Abbey was established in the 10th century, but was plundered and substantially damaged by a band of marauding Vikings in 997 AD.

After piecing together fragments of manuscripts, it came to light that in restoring the Abbey, Ordulf, Earl of Devon, was helped by local workers. To reward them, the Benedictine monks fed them with bread, clotted cream, and strawberry preserves.

And thus, the cream tea was born!

The Devonshire Split is a yeast-raised bun and traditionally is filled with thick local cream and home-made strawberry jam. Black treacle (molasses) is sometimes used instead of jam, and then they are known as "Thunder and Lightning" splits.

Just lovely!

INGREDIENTS

Makes 24 small splits

- 3 tbsp. (40g) butter

- 1-1¼ cups (240-300 ml) milk

- 3½ cups (450g) all-purpose (plain) flour

- ½ tsp. salt

- 14g dried easy-bake yeast (2 sachets)

- 2 tsp. superfine (caster) sugar

- A little extra flour for kneading

For the filling

- 1¼ cups (300ml) heavy (double) cream, softly whipped

- 8 tbsp strawberry jelly (jam) or molasses (black treacle)

METHOD

1. Melt the butter with the milk in a small pan and let it cool slightly.

2. Add the flour and salt into a large bowl and make a well in the middle. Sprinkle the yeast and superfine (caster) sugar into the well.

3. Pour the milk and butter mixture into the well and draw in the flour to form a soft dough. You may not need all the buttery milk. Knead it together to form a ball.

4. Tip the dough out onto a floured work surface and knead the dough lightly for about five minutes until it feels slightly elastic. Return it to the bowl and cover loosely with a clean tea towel and put in a warm place to rise.

5. After an hour or so, the dough should have doubled in size. Turn the dough out on to the floured board and cut into 24 equal pieces. I cut the dough into quarters and then each quarter into six. Knead each piece into a ball and place on a lightly greased baking sheet.

6. Preheat the oven to 400°F (200°C).

7. Leave the buns to rise slightly, covered by a tea towel, for 10-15 minutes. Bake for 15 minutes until they are pale gold on top and sound somewhat hollow when tapped on the bottom.

8. Remove the buns from the baking sheet to a cooling rack for a few minutes.

9. Slice each bun diagonally not quite all the way through and fill each with a teaspoon of jelly (jam) or black treacle (molasses) and whipped cream.

One is just not enough!

Continuing southwest some 87 miles into the most western county of England, Cornwall, we arrive in Truro to sample the Cornish Hevva Cake.

8. CORNISH HEVVA CAKE

INTRODUCTION

The current Duchess of Cornwall is Camilla, the wife of the Prince of Wales, Prince Charles. Although Camilla is legally entitled to the title Princess of Wales, she chose to use Duchess of Cornwall out of respect for Charles' late wife, Princess Diana.

Every summer, the Duke and Duchess of Cornwall tour Devon and Cornwall and, very often, their tour coincides with the Duchess' birthday, 17th July, which is an excellent occasion for tea and cakes!

Cornwall has its own language, Cornish. It is one of six Celtic languages and is trying to be revived in Cornwall today.

Cornwall is a peninsular county and has the longest coastline in Britain: 433 miles. The area has over 300 beaches with great surfing to help build up an appetite for this treat!

FUN FACTS

The Phoenicians from the Eastern Mediterranean, where Lebanon is today, visited Cornwall over 2,000 years ago. They were a great nation of seafarers and traders.

When the Phoenicians came to Cornwall to trade for tin, they brought with them some of the dried fruits that they loved, and which we still enjoy today.

Legend has it that the miners of Cornwall had Cornish pasties, which are meat and vegetable-filled pastries, but the fishermen had the heavy cake or heave cake. The story goes that the fishermen were hauling in their nets crying "heave-ho", which was the signal for their wives to begin preparing the "heave-ho" cake for their tea. The cake then became known as heavy or hevva cake.

The hevva cake shouldn't have any raising agent or eggs, and you might think that it would be stodgy and heavy - but it isn't - just rather delicious.

INGREDIENTS

Makes about 34

- 5½ cups (680g) all-purpose (plain) flour

- ½ tsp. of salt

- 1 cup (225g) butter

- ½ cup (100g) superfine (caster) sugar

- 3⅓ cups (500g) currants - never anything but currants

- 1 cup (150g) chopped mixed peel or candied (optional)

- 1¾ cup (425 ml) of cold water

- Sprinkling of superfine (caster) sugar

METHOD

1. Preheat the oven to 400°F (200°C) and grease a baking sheet.

2. Place the flour in a large bowl and mix in the salt.

3. Rub the butter into the flour until it's the texture of fine breadcrumbs.

4. Add the sugar, currants, and mixed or candied peel if using and mix well.

5. Add the water and mix to a soft, stiff dough.

6. Roll out the mixture or flattern with your hands and transfer to the baking sheet pushing down firmly into the corners. Score the top of the cake with a sharp knife, making crisscross, diagonal lines.

7. Place in the middle of the preheated oven and bake for 30 minutes, or until golden brown and a skewer inserted in the center comes out clean.

8. Remove from the oven and, while still warm, give a generous sprinkling of superfine (caster) sugar. Allow to cool a little and cut through your previous scoring into slices.

We will travel about 169 miles northeast back through Devon into the county of Somerset and to Bath, named after its famous Roman Baths and Pump Room to sample the Bath Bun.

9. BATH BUNS

INTRODUCTION

Bath derives its name from the famous Roman baths built in 43 BC. It became a city in 1585 AD when Queen Elizabeth I declared it to be so.

Bath is also the city of Jane Austin, and according to the Jane Austin society, she loved the Bath Bun! She would often sneak them into her lodgings to supplement her meager food offerings.

FUN FACTS

Originally Bath Buns were made without fruit but with added spices. Caraway comfits, which are sugar-coated caraway seeds, were used as an ingredient and to decorate the bun. Caraway seeds date from a 1769 AD recipe and do add a sensational note to the buns.

I love caraway as it has a sweet, warm aroma with a flavor like aniseed and fennel. In Elizabethan times it was used to flavor bread, cakes, and fruit, particularly apples. It is popular with English tea in a seed cake like a pound cake served warm with butter.

These Bath Buns are sweet yeast-raised buns, containing fruits, topped with coarse white sugar crystals and caraway seeds.

INGREDIENTS

Makes 12

- 3½ cups (450g) all-purpose (plain) flour

- 1 tsp. salt

- ⅔ cup (150g) butter (unsalted, at room temperature)

- 7g sachet of instant yeast

- 2 tbsp. superfine (caster) sugar

- 1 tbsp. caraway seeds (generous portion)

- 1 cup (240 ml) milk (lukewarm)

For the Topping:

- 2 tbsp. sugar mixed with 2 tbsp. water

- 3 sugar cubes (white, roughly crushed)

- 1 tbsp. caraway seeds

METHOD

1. Place the flour in a large bowl and add the salt.

2. Rub in the butter until it is like coarse breadcrumbs.

3. Make a well in the center and sprinkle into the well the yeast, sugar, and caraway seeds, and mix.

4. Warm the milk and stir it into the dry ingredients to give a soft dough.

5. Knead the dough for about five minutes on a floured surface until it is smooth and pliable.

Return it to the bowl and cover loosely with a clean tea towel and put in a warm place to rise.

6. After about an hour, knock the air out of the dough and divide it into 12 equal pieces. Knead and form 12 buns, put onto greased baking sheets, cover with a damp tea towel, and leave to rise again for up to 1 hour.

7. About 10 minutes before the end of the rising time, preheat your oven to 375°F (190°C).

8. Bake for 12–15 minutes until they are golden brown.

For the Topping: Heat together the sugar and water for the glaze, and brush it over the hot buns, then strew the crushed sugar cubes and caraway seeds over the top.

Eat them warm or cold, as they are or with butter if you fancy.

We are staying in Bath for another type of bun, steeped in history and myth, the Sally Lunn Bun.

10. SALLY LUNN BUNS

INTRODUCTION

Hidden beneath the city of Bath is an incredible Roman bath complex. Constructed in around 70 AD as a grand bathing and socializing complex, the Roman Baths is one of the best-preserved Roman remains in the world, where 1,170,000 liters of steaming spring water, reaching 115°F (46°C), still fills the bathing site every single day.

The baths are surrounded by 18th- and 19th-century buildings but, the original Roman main bath had walls reaching some 40m and would have been magnificent.

FUN FACTS

The name Sally Lunn belongs to the woman who first made this bread in Bath. She was a pastry cook who owned a shop in Lilliput Alley.

Sally Lunn sold her cakes to the wealthy and fashionable who came to Bath to sample the waters, and they were eaten in the pump room of the baths.

The story goes that Sally Lunn was a Huguenot refugee (perhaps better known as Solange Luyon) who came to Bath in 1680 AD via Bristol after escaping persecution in France.

In Lilliput Alley, she found work with a baker and introduced her now-famous light and delicate bun to pre-Georgian Bath. The basement of the house has a venerable oven dating from 1137 AD, and it is said that is where she baked her buns.

Sally's fame, together with that of her bun, grew and grew alongside the reputation of the city of Bath. The original and very secret recipe was passed on with the deeds to Sally Lunn's house. The buns are still made by hand at Sally Lunn's Eating House today, where you can sample them with all manner of different toppings. Having visited myself, I can say it is well worth a visit!

This bread should be eaten split in two and spread generously with butter.

INGREDIENTS

Makes 18

- 1 cup (240 ml) whole milk

- ¼ cup (50g) superfine (caster) sugar

- 1 stick or ½ cup (100g) butter

- 3½ cups (450g) all-purpose (plain) flour

- 1½ tsp. salt

- 1 tbsp. instant yeast or 7g sachet

- Zest of 1 lemon

- 2 large eggs

- ½ cup (75g) dried fruit, e.g., golden raisins (optional)

- Beaten egg to brush on top

METHOD

1. Mix the milk and sugar in a small bowl.

2. Melt the butter and add it to the sugary milk.

3. In a large bowl, mix together the flour and salt.

4. Make a well in the flour and add the buttery, sugary milk, sprinkle on the yeast, lemon zest, and add the eggs.

5. Mix together, and if you are using the dried fruit, add them here.

6. Knead for a few minutes.

7. Cover and leave to rise for about an hour somewhere warm.

8. After about an hour, knock the air out of the dough and divide into 18 equal pieces. Knead and form 18 buns, put onto greased baking sheets, cover with a damp tea towel, and leave to rise again for up to 1 hour.

9. About 10 minutes before the end of the rising time, preheat your oven to 350°F (180°C).

10. Brush the risen rolls with beaten egg to glaze and bake for 15-20 minutes in a preheated oven.

Eat warm cut in half with butter. Hmmm!

We now travel north for 76 miles to Hereford for our next recipe, Herefordshire Cider Cake.

11. HEREFORDSHIRE CIDER CAKE

INTRODUCTION

On arriving in Hereford, the county town of Herefordshire, you are greeted by the stunning Cathedral.

This Cathedral houses the Magna Carta, which was agreed between King John and his barons at Runnymede in 1215 AD and is one of the most preeminent documents in history. The right of the freedom of the individual or habeas corpus is famously contained in the American Bill of Rights embodied in the constitution of the United States of America.

The Cathedral also houses the 13th Century Mappa Mundi which, is the most important and most celebrated medieval map in any form. It is drawn on a single sheet of vellum (calfskin) and reflects the thinking of the medieval Church with Jerusalem at the center of the world.

FUN FACTS

Local cooks began experimenting with using cider in cooking with the opening of what became the world's largest cider-making factory in Hereford in 1887 AD. To this day, this cake is eaten all year round and is celebrated at the annual cider festival in Ross on Wye in Herefordshire each August.

This is a beautifully moist cake flavored with nutmeg and cider.

INGREDIENTS

Serves 16

- ⅔ cup (150g) butter

- ¾ cup (150g) superfine (caster) sugar

- 1¾ cups (315g) self-rising (self-raising) flour

- 1½ tsp. baking soda (bicarbonate of soda)

- 2 tsp. grated nutmeg

- 3 large eggs

- 1¼ cups (300ml) cider

- Superfine (caster) sugar for dusting

- 9" (23cm) square cake pan

METHOD

1. Preheat the oven to 350°F (180°C).

2. Line your cake pan with greased baking parchment.

3. Melt the butter in a medium saucepan.

4. Add the sugar, flour, baking soda (bicarbonate of soda), and nutmeg.

5. Beat in the eggs and cider and thoroughly mix.

6. Pour into the prepared pan (it is quite runny).

7. Bake in the oven for 30-35 minutes.

8. Remove from the pan and sprinkle with superfine (caster) sugar.

9.   Cut into squares when cool.

Traveling northeast 78 miles brings us to Coventry, the most central city in the whole of England, where we will sample some Coventry Godcakes.

12. COVENTRY GODCAKES

INTRODUCTION

The original Cathedral in Coventry was built in the 14th century. Sadly, Coventry suffered severe bomb damage during the Second World War. The present Coventry Cathedral was rebuilt mainly after the majority of the 14th-century Cathedral was destroyed by the Luftwaffe in the Coventry Blitz of 14th November 1940. All that was left was a shell and the spire.

The Cathedral re-opened in 1962 and has been a real drive for reconciliation and peace. It is an extraordinary building. It seems fitting to make these Godcakes in such an atmosphere.

FUN FACTS

Coventry Godcakes have a tradition of at least 700 years. They are triangular turnovers whose three points represented the Holy Trinity, as did the three slashes across the top of the pastry.

The custom of giving Godcakes dates to pre-Reformation (16th century) Coventry. Every New Year, godparents would gift a Godcake to their godchildren as a blessing for the year to come. Sizes and prices of the pastries differed depending on the budget of the godparents. It meant that Godcakes were an accessible tradition for all social classes. The wealthier the giver, the more elaborate the cakes. Every family tried to out-do the others, which was not exactly a Christian attitude!

INGREDIENTS

Makes 12

- 13.2 oz. (375g) ready-rolled puff pastry

- 1 cup (225g) mincemeat or raspberry, strawberry or apricot jelly (jam)

- 1 beaten egg

- 1 tbsp. granulated sugar to sprinkle

- 2 greased baking sheets

METHOD

1. Preheat the oven to 425°F (220°C).

2. Unroll the ready-rolled pastry. You are aiming for 24 similar-sized triangles. I find it easiest to cut the pastry into three equal strips longways and then cut each strip into 4 squares. This gives you 12 squares. Each square can then be cut diagonally in half, giving you 24 triangles in all.

3. Take 2 greased baking sheets and place 6 triangles on each baking sheet, nicely spaced.

4. Put a teaspoon of mincemeat or jelly (jam) in the middle of each triangle.

5. Wet the edges and cover each triangle with one of the plain pastry triangles and gently press down the edges to seal.

6. Brush the tops with beaten egg, make three slits on the top and sprinkle with granulated sugar.

7. Bake for 12-15 minutes until golden brown.

Serve warm with a dollop of cream, or if you have any godchildren, perhaps invite them over and let them enjoy!

We travel 19 miles north to the town of Market Bosworth, home to the battle of Bosworth Field and the Bosworth Jumbles.

13. BOSWORTH JUMBLES

INTRODUCTION

The Battle of Bosworth was the final battle between two warring houses, the House of Tudor and the House of Lancaster. This battle resulted in the death of Richard III and the victory of Henry, who became Henry IV. Both houses had a rose as their emblem, so the war is known as the War of the Roses.

Incredibly, the remains of Richard III were discovered under a parking lot in 2012 and have been reinterred in Leicester Cathedral, 14 miles East of Bosworth. There is also the Richard III visitor center 100 yards from the Cathedral.

FUN FACTS

The word Jumble is thought to come from "gemmel," meaning a twin finger ring because the early jumbles were often in the form of two interlaced rings. The recipe is said, perhaps rather fancifully, to have been found in the hand of Richard III's dead cook on the battlefield where Richard III was killed, and his army routed by Henry Tudor in 1485 AD.

Jumbles were first written about in Elizabethan times and were flavored with aniseed or caraway seeds. Almond flavor jumbles have been popular since the 17th century.

INGREDIENTS

Makes 16

- 2½ cups (300g) self-rising (self-raising) flour

- ⅓ cup (60g) rice flour

- 1 cup (200g) superfine (caster) sugar

- 1 cup or 2 sticks (220g) butter

- 1 egg

- 1 tsp. almond essence or 2 tsp. crushed caraway seeds

- 1 tbsp. milk if needed

- 2 greased baking sheets

METHOD

1. Preheat the oven to 350°F (180°C).

2. Mix the self-rising (self-raising) flour, rice flour, and sugar in a large bowl.

3. Rub in the butter.

4. Stir in the egg and almond essence or crushed caraway seeds to form a dough. Keep mixing it together and add 1 tablespoon of milk if the dough is not forming.

5. Divide the dough in half and put one half in the fridge while you work with the other half.

6. Roll out half the dough into a rectangle about 12 x 8 inches (32 x 20cm).

7. Cut 16 strips of dough from the rectangle. I find it easiest to cut it into quarters and then each quarter into 4 strips. That way, it is easier to get the strips fairly even.

8. Take a strip and cut in half, so you have two strips about 4 inches (10 cm) long. Form a circle with one half and seal by dampening the ends together. Make another circle with the other

half and interlock it with the first circle to form two interlocked rings. Carefully transfer to one of the baking sheets with a fish slice. Continue until you have made 8.

9. Repeat the process with the other half of dough from the fridge, so you have 2 sheets with 8 Bosworth Jumbles on each.

10. Place both sheets in the oven and bake for about 10 minutes.

11. While hot sprinkle with superfine (caster) sugar and carefully transfer each jumble to a cooling rack.

Serve with a nice cup of tea. If you have used the caraway seeds, you will find a gentle hint of aniseed flavor.

Sixty-four miles west brings us to Shrewsbury, in Shropshire. This is home to the Shrewsbury Biscuit, which we shall taste next.

14. SHREWSBURY BISCUITS

We have traveled on our journey so far west that we are now only 9 miles east of the Welsh border.

Shrewsbury town center has a largely unspoiled medieval street plan with about 660 listed buildings of importance.

The town was given to Roger de Montgomery as a gift from William the Conqueror after the successful invasion in 1066 AD. Montgomery, who was one of William the Conqueror's trusted counselors, built Shrewsbury Castle in 1074 AD, which is a striking red sandstone castle. He also founded Shrewsbury Abbey as a Benedictine monastery in 1083 AD.

The Abbey's windows and walls still bear the marks of musket-shot from Cromwell's troops from about 1645 AD.

Both the Abbey and the Castle can still be visited today.

FUN FACTS

Shrewsbury biscuits were first mentioned in a recipe book dated 1658 AD.

The Shrewsbury Biscuit is thought to have developed from an original recipe for Shrewsbury Cake, and one of the most renowned recipes was produced by a Mr. Palin in 1760 AD. In Shrewsbury Castle Foregate there is a plaque referring to Mr. Palin which says:

"Oh! Palin, Prince of Cake Compounders,

The mouth liquefies at thy very name!

They are mouth-watering!"

Another surprising fact is that Shrewsbury Biscuits are among the most popular snacks in India!

INGREDIENTS

Makes 24

- ½ cup or 1 stick (125g) butter, room temperature
- ¾ cup (150g) superfine (caster) sugar
- 1 large egg
- 1¾ cup (225g) all-purpose (plain) flour
- Zest of 1 lemon
- ⅓ cup (50g) currants
- Superfine (caster) sugar to sprinkle.
- 2¼ inch (6 cm) biscuit cutter and two baking sheets.

METHOD

1. Preheat the oven to 350°F (180°C).

2. Squash together the butter and sugar until they are amalgamated and then beat together. (No need for a mixer.)

3. Add the egg with a tablespoon of the flour and beat well.

4. Stir in the rest of the flour, lemon zest and currants and mix to a firm dough.

5. Turn onto a lightly floured surface and roll out to a thickness of about 5 mm.

6. Cut into rounds with a 2¼ inch (6cm) biscuit cutter and place on two large greased baking sheets. Makes about 24.

7. Bake for 13-15 minutes, until firm and light brown.

8. While still hot sprinkle with superfine (caster) sugar.

We drive 68 miles northeast to the town of Bakewell in Derbyshire. As you can probably guess - it's the home of the Bakewell Tart.

15. BAKEWELL TART

INTRODUCTION

Thinly disguised as 'Lambton' in Jane Austen's Pride and Prejudice, Bakewell is the ideal place for a stroll around the mellow stone buildings, medieval five-arched stone bridge, and quaint courtyards.

While revising Pride & Prejudice – staying, it's believed, at the Rutland Arms in Bakewell – she wrote: 'There is not a finer county in England than Derbyshire.'

FUN FACTS

Originally called Bakewell pudding and was allegedly made by mistake! The Landlady of the White Horse Inn (since demolished) left instructions for a maid to make a jam tart, but instead of mixing the almond paste and eggs into the pastry, she spread it on top of the jam; thus, the Bakewell Tart was created.

Though the first recipe dates from the late 1800s, the idea of this tart is much more ancient. In medieval times, ground almonds and sugar were used to make a paste called marchpane, which is not unlike the topping for this tart.

Bakewell Tart is served either at teatime with a cup of tea, or even as a dessert with custard. Traditionally, it has sliced, or flaked almonds scattered on top but the tart has become popular with icing instead of the sliced almonds. So do choose what you would prefer or use both!

A variation adopted by many cooks uses strawberry jelly (jam) instead of raspberry. Both work very well.

INGREDIENTS

Serves 8

- 13.2 oz. (375g) shortcrust pastry to line 9 inch (23 cm) removable bottom cake pan or a pre-baked pastry case

- ½ cup (125g) butter

- ⅔ cup (125g) superfine (caster) sugar

- 1¼ cup (125g) ground almonds

- 1 tsp. almond extract

- 2 large eggs

- 4 tbsp. raspberry jelly (jam)

- 1½ tbsp. (50g) sliced or flaked almonds (optional)

METHOD

1. Preheat the oven to 350°F (180°C) and place a baking sheet in the oven to heat.

2. Line your 9-inch (23 cm) cake pan with shortcrust pastry and bake it blind (See Appendix - Pastry Tips for how to do this). Or use a pre-baked pastry case.

3. Cream together the butter and the sugar until light and fluffy.

4. Beat in the eggs, one at a time.

5. Stir in the almond extract and the ground almonds.

6. Spread the raspberry jelly (jam) over the base of your tart.

7. Carefully spread over the almond mixture. It does look unpromising, but it will be delicious.

8. Sprinkle with the almonds, if using, and bake on the preheated baking sheet in the oven for about 35-40 minutes.

Once the tart has cooled a little, serve with ice-cream or cream.

Sixty-six miles west brings us to Chester, which was founded as a Roman fort in 79 AD.

It is here that we shall taste another tart, though not so well-known as the Bakewell Tart, it's called Chester Tart.

16. CHESTER TART

INTRODUCTION

The name Chester is derived from the Latin meaning fortress or walled town. It was home to one of the three Roman legions stationed in Britain in the 70s AD.

Chester is a walled city in Cheshire. It boasts the most complete city walls, the oldest racecourse, and the largest Roman Amphitheater in Britain. It also has a stunning Cathedral dating back to 1092 AD with Europe's finest example of medieval carvings. It was built to celebrate God's presence in the world.

FUN FACTS

This tart is made with shortcrust pastry, filled with a lemony custard and topped with meringue. It is an early Victorian version of a lemon meringue pie. How the pie came to be called Chester pie seems lost in time. However, I like to imagine that this tart or pie was served frequently by the good people of Chester, and hence took on the city's name.

Even though it is like a lemon meringue pie, this tart has a slightly thicker lemon layer, and the addition of almonds really makes a delectable change.

INGREDIENTS

Serves 8

- 13.2 oz. (375g) shortcrust pastry to line 9 inch (23 cm) removable bottom cake pan or a pre-baked pastry case

- 6 tbsp. (85g) butter

- Zest and juice of 1 lemon

- ½ cup (100g) granulated sugar

- 4 egg yolks

- 4 tbsp. ground almonds

For the meringue topping:

- 4 egg whites

- ½ cup (100g) superfine (caster) sugar

METHOD

1. Line the cake pan with pastry and bake blind (See Appendix - Pastry Tips for how to do this) or use a pre-baked pastry case.

2. Preheat the oven to 350°F (180°C).

3. Melt the butter in a small saucepan and remove from the heat.

4. Whisk in the lemon zest and juice, granulated sugar, and four egg yolks followed by the ground almonds.

5. Return to the heat and stir until the mixture thickens but do not allow to boil.

6. Pour into the prepared pastry case and leave to cool. Meanwhile, make the meringue topping.

7. Whisk the egg whites until stiff. Whisk in half the superfine (caster) sugar and whisk again until glossy and stiff. Fold in the remaining sugar. Pile on top of the tart.

8. Bake in the preheated oven for 5 minutes.

9. Then reduce the heat to 325°F (160°C) and bake for another 20-30 minutes until golden brown on top. The lemon layer will be beautifully set.

Serve warm or cold, with cream for a real treat.

From the lovely city of Chester, we travel north for 18 miles and arrive in Liverpool for another tart, the Liverpool Tart.

17. LIVERPOOL TART

INTRODUCTION

The River Mersey reaches the Irish Sea at Liverpool. The origins of the city of Liverpool can be traced back to 1207 AD when a new borough was established by King John on issuing letters patent advertising "Livpul."

Of course, it is famous for football and the Beatles as well!

FUN FACTS

This pastry tart has the unusual pairing of dark muscovado sugar and lemon. As Liverpool was and is a bustling port, it is thought that the tart has its origins as a way of introducing vitamin C to sailors before they set sail to help keep scurvy at bay on their long voyages. In any event, it has a flavor like no other, which is quite intriguing.

I have adapted the original recipe, which was extremely bitter. I hope you will love this one. It has the added advantage of not even needing the pastry to be cooked before adding the filling. Though you can use a pre-baked pastry tart case and fill it anyway and it will be delicious!

INGREDIENTS

Serves 8

- 13.2 oz. (375g) shortcrust pastry to line 9 inch (23cm) removable bottom cake pan or a pre-baked pastry case

- 1 large lemon

- ⅓ cup (85g) butter

- 2½ cups (340g) dark brown sugar

- 2 large eggs

METHOD

1. Preheat the oven to 375°F (190°C) and place a baking sheet in the oven to heat.

2. Line your 9-inch (23 cm) cake pan with shortcrust pastry - no need to "blind" bake and leave to chill in the fridge. Or use a pre-baked pastry case.

3. Remove the pips from the lemon and whizz it all up in a processor or chop it all into very small pieces.

4. Melt the butter and mix with the sugar.

5. Combine the butter mixture with whizzed lemon and the eggs.

6. Remove the hot baking sheet from the oven and place your pastry cake pan from the fridge on it.

7. Carefully pour in the filling mixture - it will be quite runny, and that's fine.

8. Place the baking sheet with the cake pan in the oven for about 20-25 minutes until set and brown.

Leave to cool and serve warm or cold with cream or ice cream.

Driving east 34 miles takes us to Manchester, and here we shall sample the Manchester Tart.

18. MANCHESTER TART

INTRODUCTION

The first recorded civilian settlement in the area was about 79 AD, where it was associated with a Roman fort on a sandstone bluff.

But Roman forts may not be the first thing you think of when you hear the name Manchester - it may be the two famous football clubs, Manchester United and Manchester City. Both are in the Premier League, and games between the clubs are referred to as the Manchester Derby.

During the Industrial Revolution, Manchester was, for a time, the most productive center of cotton processing and became known as the world's largest marketplace for cotton goods. It was called "Cottonopolis" and "Warehouse City" during the Victorian era.

When the Manchester Ship Canal opened in January 1894, it was the largest navigation canal in the world. The canal, a 36-mile-long (58 km) inland waterway which linked Manchester to the Irish Sea, enabled the newly created Port of Manchester to become Britain's third busiest port despite being some 36 miles inland.

FUN FACTS

The Victorian food writer, Mrs. Beeton, records a recipe for Manchester Pudding involving pastry, jam, and a lemony custard topping. It may be that the tart comes from that.

However, my favorite story of the origins of the tart is of a school chef who overcooked a batch of custard tarts. To make them more appetizing to a hall full of schoolchildren, he sprinkled some coconut on top, and when asked what the dessert was called, said Manchester Tart as it was the first name that came to mind!

A common variation is a layer of thinly sliced bananas under the custard.

INGREDIENTS

Serves 8

- 13.2 oz. (375g) shortcrust pastry to line 9 inch (23 cm) removable bottom cake pan or a pre-baked pastry case

- 2 cups (500ml) full-fat milk

- 3 tbsp. custard powder

- 2 tbsp. superfine (caster) sugar

- 1 tsp. vanilla extract

- 4 tbsp. raspberry jelly (jam)

- 5 tbsp. desiccated coconut

METHOD

1. Line the cake pan with pastry and bake blind (See Appendix - Pastry Tips for how to do this) or use a pre-baked pastry case.

2. Mix a few tablespoons of the milk with the custard powder and sugar to make a paste.

3. Pour the milk into a saucepan, add the vanilla extract, and the custard mixture.

4. Stir with a whisk over the heat until it has thickened nicely. The whisk will stop it from getting lumpy.

5. Leave the custard to cool slightly.

6. Take your pastry shell and spread with the raspberry jelly (jam).

7. Sprinkle over about half of the coconut.

8. Carefully pour over the custard.

9. Sprinkle over the remaining coconut and put it in the fridge to chill and set for at least an hour.

Serve with cream or ice-cream.

Eccles lies only 5 miles west of Manchester city center. Let's go there to taste some delicious Eccles Cakes.

19. ECCLES CAKES

INTRODUCTION

Eccles was on the route of the world's first passenger railway, the Liverpool and Manchester Railway. This railway was the first inter-city railway in the world. Opening on 15th September 1830 between the towns of Liverpool and Manchester, it provided a high-speed link between these two Lancashire towns.

It was the first railway to be entirely double-tracked throughout its length, the first to have a signaling system, the first to be fully timetabled, and the first to carry mail.

Eccles expanded along the route.

FUN FACTS

Eccles cakes were first produced in 1796 AD and are now exported across the world.

These cakes use puff pastry, and unlike some foods, like Cornish clotted cream, it has not been granted Protected Geographical Indication status by the EU, and so can be made and sold anywhere and still called an Eccles Cake. So, wherever you are, have a go at these!

INGREDIENTS

Makes 12

- 13.2 oz. (375g) ready-rolled puff pastry

For the filling:

- ⅛ cup (25g) butter

- ⅓ cup (60g) light brown sugar

- ¾ cup (100g) currants

- Zest of 1 orange

- ½ tsp. pumpkin (mixed) spice

For the topping:

- 1 beaten egg

- 2 tbsp. granulated sugar

METHOD

1. Preheat the oven to 400°F (200°C).

2. Melt the butter and mix all the filling ingredients together.

3. Unroll the pastry and cut it into 3 lengthways and then cut each strip into 4, giving you 12 squares, each approximately 3-inch (8 cm) square.

4. Place a heaped teaspoonful of filling in the middle of each square.

5. Dampen the edges of the pastry with water and bring them together to seal.

6. Turn each cake over and nicely shape with your hands into a flattish circle and place on the baking sheet.

7. Slash three incisions on the top of each cake, brush with egg, and sprinkle with the granulated sugar.

8. Bake for 15-20 minutes until golden brown.

Serve warm or cold. Delicious for a packed lunch treat.

Traveling 22 miles northwest, we arrive in Chorley, ready for tasting the Chorley Cakes.

20. CHORLEY CAKES

INTRODUCTION

The name, Chorley, comes from the Anglo-Saxon word meaning a clearing in a woodland. It was heavily wooded in those times.

One of the pilgrim fathers was called Myles Standish and he was born in Duxbury Hall, Chorley. It is thought to be the reason behind why the seaside town of Duxbury in Massachusetts is so named. As 2020 marks 400 years since the Mayflower set sail, the town of Chorley celebrated the life of Myles Standish. Maybe he packed some of these delicious cakes to fortify him on his voyage?

FUN FACTS

A Chorley Cake used to be an addition to a working man's lunch box. It was often eaten with a spread of butter on the top or with some Lancashire cheese. I love the influences of medieval cooking with the sweet and salty combination which still permeate our recipes today. Try it, very simple, but such a treat.

It uses shortcrust pastry and is a delicious combination of currants and sugar.

INGREDIENTS

Makes 12

- 13.2 oz. (375g) shortcrust pastry or ready-rolled shortcrust pastry
- 1 cup (150g) currants
- ¼ cup (50g) superfine (caster) sugar
- 1 small egg for glazing the tops

METHOD

1. Preheat the oven to 400°F (200°C).

2. Mix the currants and the sugar together.

3. Roll out your shortcrust pastry to about ⅕ inch (0.5 cm) thick.

4. Cut large circles 3½ inches (9 cm) out of the pastry.

5. Fill each circle with about a tablespoon of currant mixture.

6. Bring the edges of the circle together and seal and turn the parcel over so the seal is underneath.

7. Roll each cake with your rolling pin so that the currants just begin to show through.

8. With the leftover pastry, roll out and repeat the above process.

9. Place all these flat cakes on a baking sheet and brush the tops with the beaten egg.

10. Bake in the oven for 15 minutes until golden brown.

Leave to cool on a cooling rack and enjoy with butter, or cheese, or on their own.

Thirty miles north takes us to Lancaster for our Lancaster Lemon Tart.

21. LANCASTER LEMON TART

INTRODUCTION

On arrival, your view will be dominated by the 12th-century Castle on a hill, Lancaster Castle, which astonishingly, until 2011, was a fully functioning HM Prison!

The Castle has been a center for criminal justice, penal reform, and incarceration for almost 1,000 years. It is one of the most important surviving historic buildings in the country. The Castle is often called John O'Gaunt's Castle, who was the Duke of Lancaster from 1377-1399 AD. O'Gaunt was great friends with Chaucer, who famously wrote The Canterbury Tales in 1392 AD.

There is a Lancastrian toast, 'The Queen, Duke of Lancaster!' which refers to Her Majesty, the Queen. But, hold on, I hear you cry, surely a Duke has to be male, shouldn't it be, "The Queen, Duchess of Lancaster"? Well, you would be right ordinarily, except for this Dukedom!

John O'Gaunt's son Henry Bolingbroke became King Henry IV, and he passed a Royal Charter in 1399 AD, which decreed that the Duchy should be a distinct entity held separate from all other Crown possessions and handed down through the Monarchy.

That is precisely what happens to this day. The Monarch is always the Duke of Lancaster, whether King or Queen. So the Lancastrian toast 'The Queen, Duke of Lancaster!' referring to Her Majesty the Queen, is quite correct!

FUN FACTS

As lemons are high in Vitamin C, it may be that because Lancaster is a port town, this was a way of increasing sailors' intake of vitamin C for their sea voyages. It would reduce the risk of scurvy.

It is not necessary to pre-bake the pastry. However, if you are after a crispy bottom, then feel free to do so. It is like a Bakewell Tart but uses lemon curd instead of jam, which gives it an entirely different feel.

INGREDIENTS

Serves 8

- 13.2 oz. (375g) shortcrust pastry to line a 9 inch (23 cm) removable bottom cake pan or a ready-baked pastry case

- ½ cup (125g) butter

- ⅔ cup (125g) superfine (caster) sugar

- 1¼ cup (125g) ground almonds

- ½ tsp. almond extract

- 2 large eggs

- 4 tbsp. lemon curd

- 1½ tbsp. (50g) sliced or flaked almonds

METHOD

1. Preheat the oven to 350°F (180°C) and place a baking sheet in the oven to heat.

2. Line your 9-inch (23 cm) cake pan with shortcrust pastry and bake it blind (See Appendix - Pastry Tips for how to do this). Or use a pre-baked pastry case.

3. Cream together the butter and the sugar until light and fluffy.

4. Beat in the eggs, one at a time.

5. Stir in the almond extract and the ground almonds.

6. Spread the lemon curd over the base of your tart.

7. Carefully spread over the almond mixture. It does look unpromising, but it will be delicious.

8. Sprinkle with the almonds, if using, and bake on the preheated baking sheet in the oven for about 35-40 minutes.

Once the tart has cooled a little, serve with ice-cream or cream.

Continuing to travel north some 66 miles takes us to Carlisle in the county of Cumbria, ready to taste a slice of Cumberland Rum Nicky.

22. CUMBERLAND RUM NICKY

INTRODUCTION

The first record of the term "Cumberland" appeared in 945 AD when the Anglo-Saxon Chronicle recorded that the area was given to Malcolm I of Scotland by King Edmund of England.

The names Cumberland and Cumbria are derived from kombroges in Common Britannic, which was an ancient Celtic language, which meant "compatriots." In 1086 AD, at the time of the Domesday Book, most of the future county of Cumberland remained part of Scotland.

Cumberland existed as a separate county until 1974, and from then it became part of the county of Cumbria. Cumbria is the most sparsely populated county in England, though it is the third-largest in area. Its borders stretch to Scotland.

FUN FACTS

Cumberland Rum Nicky is stuffed with dates, sugar, and rum. Probably first becoming popular when Cumbrian Ports regularly received ships from the Caribbean, which brought in the dates, sugar, and rum. If you don't fancy using the rum, you can use rum flavoring instead.

It could be called "Nicky" due to the appearance of nicks or cuts on the top of the tart.

INGREDIENTS

Serves 8

- 18 oz. (500g) shortcrust pastry to line a 9 inch (23 cm) removable bottom cake pan and for the pastry strips for the top

For the filling:

- 1⅓ cups (225g) dates, coarsely chopped

- ½ cup (100g) dried apricots, coarsely chopped

- ¼ cup (50g) stem ginger in syrup, drained and finely chopped

- ¼ cup (50 ml) dark rum or 1 tbsp. rum flavoring

- ¼ cup (50g) soft dark brown sugar

- ¼ cup or ½ stick (50g) butter, cut into ½-¾ inch (1–2 cm) cubes

For the rum butter:

- ½ cup or 1 stick (100g) butter softened

- 1 cup (225g) light brown sugar

- ⅓ cup (75 ml) dark rum or 1½ tbsp. rum flavoring

METHOD

1. Preheat the oven to 350°F (180°C) and put in a baking sheet to heat.

2. Mix all the filling ingredients, except the butter, together in a bowl. Set aside to macerate while you make the pastry and line the cake pan.

3. Line the cake pan with pastry and place it in the fridge. (See Appendix - Pastry Tips for how to do this.)

4. Roll out the remaining pastry and cut into 8 strips about ½ inch (1 cm) wide.

5. Spread the filling over the pastry in the cake pan and dot over the butter.

6. Place the pastry strips over the tart in a crisscross fashion.

7. Bake in the oven on the preheated sheet for 35-40 minutes.

For the rum butter, beat the ingredients together until smoothly mixed.

To serve, cut a generous slice of the warm tart and add a blob of rum butter to melt on top.

From Carlisle, we drive 60 miles east into the heartland of Northumberland to Newcastle upon Tyne to taste some Northumbrian Singin' Hinnies.

23. NORTHUMBRIAN SINGIN' HINNIES

INTRODUCTION

The Kingdom of Northumbria was a medieval Anglian kingdom in what is now Northern England and southeast Scotland. The name derives from the Old English Norþan-hymbre meaning "the people or province north of the Humber."

Northumbria now refers to a much smaller region corresponding to the counties of Northumberland, County Durham, and Tyne and Wear in North East England.

Rather delightfully, the name Northumbria, even though it is not the official name for the region, is kept alive in the Northumbria police and Northumbria University, and the local Environment Agency office uses the term Northumbria to describe its area.

FUN FACTS

Northumbrian Singin' Hinnies are a type of scone but are cooked on the stove. Their sweetness comes from the dried fruit and the superfine (caster) sugar that is sprinkled over them when they are cooked.

The "Singin'" part of the name comes from the way the cakes sing when the batter hits the hot pan. "Hinny" is the way the word honey is pronounced in Northumberland and is a term of endearment.

INGREDIENTS

Makes 36

- 3 cups (450g) all-purpose (plain) flour

- 2 tsp. baking powder

- Pinch of salt

- 1 cup or 2 sticks (220g) butter (cold)

- 1¼ cups (180g) currants

- 1 cup (200ml) semi-skimmed milk to form the dough

- 1 tbsp. superfine (caster) sugar to sprinkle over

- 2-inch (6 cm) biscuit cutter

METHOD

1. Tip in the flour, baking powder, and salt into a bowl.

2. Rub in the butter.

3. Add the currants.

4. Stir in the milk to form a dough.

5. Roll out the dough to about ½ inch (1 cm) deep and use a 2-inch (6 cm) cutter to cut out circles of dough. You should have about 36.

6. Heat the frying pan or griddle and smear with butter.

7. Place 6 or 7 cakes on the hot greased frying pan or griddle and cook for about 3 minutes each side.

8. Sprinkle with superfine (caster) sugar when cooked and eat warm with butter.

From Newcastle upon Tyne to York in Yorkshire is 86 miles south, and awaiting us is the Yorkshire Blueberry and Mint Pie.

24. YORKSHIRE BLUEBERRY AND MINT PIE

INTRODUCTION

"York" comes from the Viking name for the city, Jórvík. The word "Shire" is either from the Old Norseword Skyr or from Old English Scir meaning care or official charge. The "shire" suffix is locally pronounced "shuh."

There is a fabulous museum in York called the Jórvík Viking Centre. Between the years 1976-81, archaeologists revealed the houses, workshops, and backyards of the Viking-age city of Jórvík as it stood nearly 1,000 years ago. This museum is built on the very site where the excavations took place. You travel on a little train and experience the sights, sounds, and smells of ancient York by journeying through the reconstruction of Viking-age streets and immersing yourself in life as it would have been in the 10th century York. Great fun!

FUN FACTS

Yorkshire and Blueberry Mint Pie is also called Yorkshire Mucky Mouth Pie! Originally it was made with bilberries and was called Mucky Mouth because the bilberries used to stain the eaters' mouths purple! Don't worry, this recipe won't do that! I have substituted blueberries that work beautifully, though if you have access to bilberries, feel free to use those.

It has such a refreshing and original taste that it will definitely be cause for comment if you serve this to your friends. The minty flavor survives cooking and cuts through the sweetness. It's so good I couldn't resist sharing it with you!

INGREDIENTS

Serves 8

- 18 oz. (500g) shortcrust pastry (enough to line the tin and for the top of the pie)

- 2 Bramley apples, peeled and chopped, (or if unavailable, apples with a sharp taste such as Granny Smiths)

- 3½ cups (450g) blueberries

- ½ cup (110g) superfine (caster) sugar

- 2 tbsp. chopped fresh mint

Topping :

- 1 egg white

- 3½ cups (450g) powdered (icing) sugar

METHOD

1. Preheat the oven to 400°F (200°C) and put a baking sheet in the oven to heat.

2. Line your 9-inch (23 cm) removable bottom cake pan with shortcrust pastry.

3. Mix the apples, blueberries, and sugar together and pile into your pastry tart. It may seem a lot, but it will fit in!

4. Sprinkle over the chopped mint.

5. Roll out the rest of the pastry and place it on top of the tart to form the lid.

6. Seal around the edges and cut off any excess.

7. Bake in the oven for 30 minutes on your preheated baking sheet.

8. Meanwhile, for the topping, whisk the egg white until stiff and add the sugar.

9. Remove the pie from the oven after 30 minutes and coat with the topping.

10. Cook for a further 10 minutes, until golden brown.

We are going to stay in Yorkshire for the intriguingly entitled Yorkshire Fat Rascals.

25. YORKSHIRE FAT RASCALS

INTRODUCTION

Yorkshire is the largest county in England and Yorkshire's three National Parks – the North York Moors, most of the Yorkshire Dales, and part of the Peak District – account for nearly a third of the total area of National Parks in the UK.

With 2.5 miles of wall and 5 main gates—called bars —York claims the longest town walls in England. The Romans began building them around 70 AD. The walls of York have defined the historic city for centuries. Walking the walls provides changing views of the incredible York Minster, which has abided for over 1,000 years.

The Humber Bridge, in Yorkshire, is the longest single-span suspension bridge in the UK. It's also the second-longest in Europe and the seventh longest in the world.

Back to culinary delights, Yorkshire boasts a creamy type of cheese, Wensleydale cheese, which was first made in 1150 AD by French Cistercian monks who settled in the Yorkshire Dales. It features in Wallace and Gromit's animated shorts as Wallace's favorite cheese!

FUN FACTS

Fat Rascals are traditionally from Yorkshire and are a cross between a scone and a rock cake. Light, buttery and crumbly in texture, they are to be enjoyed warm from the oven or cool - but always best with a nice cup of tea!

They were first thought to be made by Elizabethan bakers, not wanting to waste the leftover pastry, so they added spices, sugar, and fruit. The "fat" is thought to come from the use of fat in the rascals - but don't worry, it's not that much fat!

Following its launch, it quickly became Bettys Café Tea Rooms in North Yorkshire's best known and best-selling bakery product, selling over 375,000 per year. Bettys now own the registered trademark for the name "fat rascal."

INGREDIENTS

Makes 16

- 1 cup or 2 sticks (220g) butter

- ⅔ cup (135g) superfine (caster) sugar

- 4 cups self-rising (self-raising) flour

- 2 tsp. pumpkin (mixed) spice

- 2 cups (300g) dried fruit (I like to use currants, but any combination will work)

- Zest of 1 orange

- Zest of 1 lemon

- 2 eggs

- 1 egg to brush on top

- 48 blanched almonds and 16 whole glacé cherries or 32 halves to decorate.

- 2 parchment-lined baking sheets

METHOD

1. Preheat the oven to 400°F (200°C).

2. Place the butter in a large saucepan and warm through until it is almost melted.

3. Line the baking sheets with parchment.

4. Add to the melted butter the sugar, flour, spice, dried fruit, orange, and lemon zest, and finally 2 eggs and thoroughly mix.

5. If the mixture is a little too crumbly, add a teaspoon or two of milk.

6. Take about a tablespoon of mixture and form it into a patty in your hand. You are aiming for about 16 Fat Rascals, so each patty should be about 2 inches (6 cm) across.

7. Place each patty on the lined baking sheets.

8. Brush with the egg wash and decorate with the blanched almonds and cherry halves to form a face.

9. Bake for about 14 minutes until golden brown.

10. Remove from the oven and leave to cool on a cooling rack.

Fifty-four miles south brings us to Gainsborough. A delightful town in Lincolnshire, home to the Gainsborough Tart.

26. GAINSBOROUGH TART

INTRODUCTION

In 868 AD, King Alfred married the daughter of the chief of the Gaini, from where Gainsborough gets its name.

The town of Gainsborough at one time served as an important port, which may seem strange as it is more than 55 miles from the North Sea. But it provided downstream access on the mighty River Trent to the Humber estuary to Hull and out to the North Sea. Gainsborough was the most inland port in England.

FUN FACTS

Gainsborough Tart has a lemony filling, finished with a chewy, sweet coconut topping. The name of the tart probably comes from the town Gainsborough, which could have enjoyed imported coconuts from Hull.

I have investigated whether the name could have derived from the celebrated English painter Thomas Gainsborough who perhaps served this tart at his house in Suffolk, Gainsborough House. But sadly, I have been unable to find any record of the tart being served at Gainsborough House, so it seems most likely to be named after the town.

INGREDIENTS

Makes 16 squares

- 13.2 oz. (375g) shortcrust pastry to line a 12 x 8-inch (30 x 20 cm) baking pan

For the lemon layer:

- ⅓ cup (75g) superfine (caster) sugar

- 1 lemon, zest and juice

- 1 large egg yolk

- 2 tsp. cornstarch (cornflour)

- ⅓ cup (90 ml) boiling water

For the topping:

- ¼ stick (25g) butter

- 1 large egg

- ¼ cup (50g) superfine (caster) sugar

- 1 cup (100g) desiccated coconut

- ¼ tsp. baking powder

- 12 x 8-inch (30 x 20 cm) baking pan

METHOD

1. Preheat the oven to 350°F (180°C).

2. Grease and line your baking pan.

3. Roll out the pastry and put a layer on the bottom of the baking pan - no need to bake blind.

4. For the lemon layer: Dissolve the sugar with the lemon zest and juice and whisk in the egg yolk, cornflour and water until thickened. Leave to cool a little.

5. For the topping: Melt the butter and add the egg, sugar, coconut and baking powder.

6. Spread the slightly cooled lemon layer over the pastry.

7. Spread the coconut topping over the lemon layer.

8. Bake for about 30 minutes.

9. Leave to cool a little and cut into 16 squares while still warm.

We leave Gainsborough and head southeast 107 miles to Cambridge in Cambridgeshire, part of the Fenlands or Fen Country to taste a slice of Fen Country Treacle Apple Cake.

27. FEN COUNTRY TREACLE APPLE CAKE

INTRODUCTION

The Fenlands are primarily in East Anglia, which included the counties of Cambridgeshire, Norfolk, and Suffolk. These were marshy areas that have now been reclaimed as low-lying agricultural land with numerous drainage ditches and humanmade rivers.

The name East Anglia derives from the Anglo-Saxon kingdom of the East Angles, a tribe whose name originated in Anglia, northern Germany.

The black peaty soil is exceptionally fertile and produces a wealth of excellent vegetables, strawberries, plums, and apples.

FUN FACTS

This recipe was noted down in 1847 by Elizabeth Garden of Redisham Hall, Suffolk. It is evocative of the black peaty fenlands as it uses black treacle or molasses and the plentiful supply of apples available.

Black treacle or molasses, a thick, sticky dark syrup made from partly refined sugar, adds a rich dark note to this recipe, which really compliments the fruity apple.

INGREDIENTS

Serves 8

- 18 oz. (500g) shortcrust pastry to line 9 inch (23 cm) removable bottom cake pan and for the top of the pie

- 3 Bramley apples or other sharp apples

- ¼ stick (25g) butter

- ½ lemon juice

- ¼ cup (50g) granulated sugar

- 2 rounded tbsp. semolina

- 2 rounded tbsp. (25g) currants

- 2 tbsp. black treacle or molasses

- Beaten egg to glaze

- 9 inch (23 cm) pie pan

METHOD

1. Preheat the oven to 400°F (200°C).

2. Peel, core, and thinly slice the apples and place them in a saucepan with the butter and lemon juice.

3. Cover and simmer gently for 10 minutes.

4. Stir in the sugar and semolina and bring slowly to the boil, then simmer for 5 minutes and leave to cool.

5. Divide the pastry in 2 and roll out one half and line the cake pan. (See Appendix-Pastry Tips for how to do this.)

6. Spread the pastry tart with half of the apple mixture.

7. Sprinkle with the currants and let the treacle or molasses drop over the mixture.

8. Top with the remaining apple mixture.

9. Roll out the other half of pastry for the lid, dampen the rim of the pastry base, cover the apple mixture with the pastry lid and seal the edges.

10. Brush the lid with the beaten egg.

11. Bake for 20-25 minutes until golden brown.

12. Serve hot or cold.

Traveling 29 miles west from Cambridge, we arrive in Bedford, Bedfordshire, for our next recipe, the Bedfordshire Clanger.

28. BEDFORDSHIRE CLANGER

INTRODUCTION

"Up the wooden hill to Bedfordshire" was a favorite expression of the middle classes in the 1930s and 1940s and is still used a little today! It means going upstairs to bed.

Dame Vera Lynn, an English singer, known as "the Forces' Sweetheart," encouraged and fortified the troops during the Second World War and sang about this in 1936:

"The old wooden hill was the old wooden stairs

and Bedfordshire of course where I knelt to say my prayers

Climbing up the wooden hill to Bedfordshire.

They were happy happy days for me."

FUN FACTS

A Bedfordshire Clanger was a traditional lunch for farm laborers. It has a savory end, usually filled with meat and vegetables, and a sweet end filled with fruit. It was the main course and a dessert in one! Traditionally made with suet crust pastry, but I'm using shortcrust, which works brilliantly.

The laborers had inventive ways to keep their clangers warm - they, allegedly, buried their wrapped clangers in the middle of a dung heap!

Interestingly this is from where the British expression "dropping a clanger" comes. It means to make a big mistake.

So, you had better not drop a clanger while going up the wooden hill to Bedfordshire!

If you are vegetarian, I suggest substituting a mixture of cooked root vegetables, such as carrots and parsnips for the ham, and proceed with the recipe.

INGREDIENTS

Makes 10

- 18 oz. (500g) shortcrust pastry

Savory filling:

- 1 tsp. oil

- 1 chopped onion

- 1½ cups (225g) chopped ham or gammon

- 1 tsp. dried sage

- 1 Bramley cooking apple or a sharp apple such as Granny Smith

- ⅓ cup (50g) cooked peas

- White pepper and salt seasoning

Sweet filling:

- 2 dessert apples, peeled, cored and chopped

- 2 tbsp. superfine (caster) sugar

- 1 orange, zest, and juice

- Glaze: 1 beaten egg

METHOD

1. Add the oil and onion to a frying pan and cook for 2-3 minutes.

2. Add the ham or gammon and sage and frequently stir for 5 minutes.

3. Add the chopped apple to the mixture and cook for a further 5 minutes before adding the peas and continue cooking for 2 more minutes. Season with white pepper and salt.

4. Leave to cool.

To make the sweet filling:

5. Cook the apple in a small pan with the sugar and zest and juice of the orange for 3 minutes until softened.

6. Leave to cool.

To put it all together:

7. Roll out the pastry into a large rectangle.

8. Cut the pastry into 10 equal rectangles, I cut the pastry in half and then each half into 5 pieces.

9. Take one of the pastry rectangles and gently draw a line with your knife down the mid-way half.

10. Cut a thin strip off one end and use as a dividing wall between savory and sweet and place it two-thirds of the way down one side of the rectangle. Hopefully, this makes sense when you see the photograph of the pre-cooked Clanger.

11. Working only on the half with the dividing wall, add a tablespoon of the savory mixture to the larger two-thirds side of the pastry and a dessertspoonful of the apple mixture to the smaller third.

12. Fold over the empty half of the pastry on top of the fillings and seal the edges.

13. Place the seal underneath.

14. Brush the pastry with a beaten egg and make 3 slashes on the sweet end, and 2 on the savory end, so that when it's cooked, you'll know which end to eat first.

15. Bake for 35 minutes until golden brown.

These are such a surprise and great for picnics or packed lunches as well as at teatime.

Let's continue our journey 46 miles west to Banbury and taste some delicious Banbury Tarts.

29. BANBURY TARTS

INTRODUCTION

Banbury is a town in Oxfordshire, England. The name Banbury derives from "Banna" a Saxon chieftain said to have built a defense fortification there in the 6th century, and "burgh" means a settlement.

Jonathan Swift stayed in the late 17th century Whateley Hall Hotel in Banbury. He is reputed to have taken the name Gulliver, which he used for his famous novel Gulliver's Travels, from a tombstone in the nearby churchyard.

FUN FACTS

A Banbury cake is a spiced, currant-filled, flat pastry cake like an Eccles cake or Chorley cake, although it is more oval. They were once exclusively made and sold in Banbury. They have been made using secret recipes since 1586 AD.

Having a similar filling to the Banbury cakes based on currants, these Banbury tarts are easy to make and have a delicious lemony moist center.

INGREDIENTS

Makes 24

- 18 oz. (500g) shortcrust pastry or ready-rolled shortcrust pastry

- ½ cup or 1 stick (110g) butter, softened

- 1½ cups (300g) granulated sugar

- 3 eggs

- 1 cup (150g) dried currants

- 1 lemon, zest, and juice

- 1 tbsp. powdered (icing) sugar to dust

- 2 x 12-hole muffin pans and a 3 inch (8 cm) fluted cutter

METHOD

1. Preheat the oven to 375°F (190°C).

2. Grease both 12-hole muffin pans.

3. Roll out the pastry and cut into circles - whatever size will fit your muffin pan, I have used a 3 inch (8 cm) fluted cutter.

4. Place each pastry round into the muffin pan.

5. In a large bowl, cream the butter and sugar together thoroughly.

6. Add eggs, currants, lemon zest and juice, and mix.

7. Place 1 heaped teaspoonful of filling in each tart case.

8. Bake in the oven for 15-20 minutes.

Delicious served warm, dusted with powdered (icing) sugar.

Let us travel 77 miles southeast back to London, where we started our journey to try our last recipe, Tottenham Cake.

30. TOTTENHAM CAKE

INTRODUCTION

We have arrived back in London, having journeyed around England sampling her wares. I hope you have enjoyed our voyage and have been encouraged to make some of the recipes and share them with friends and family. It seems appropriate to end our journey here with Tottenham Cake because the nature of this cake is one of giving, sharing, and celebrating.

Tottenham, in North London, comes from the name of a local landowner Tota as recorded in the Doomsday book in 1086 AD. Tota's hamlet, it is thought, developed into Tottenham. There has been a settlement in Tottenham for at least 1,000 years.

FUN FACTS

Tottenham Cake is a type of tray-baked sponge cake, topped with pink icing, and it has a heady fragrance due to the raspberries or mulberries used to color the icing.

Local baker Henry Chalky first produced the cake in about 1901. Each slice was sold for one penny, with offcuts sold for a halfpenny. The lurid pink icing comes from the mulberries, which are grown in the Quaker Meeting House garden. It ties in very well with the Quaker ideals of simplicity and equality as it can be easily cut up and distributed.

In 1901, free slices of cake were distributed to local children to celebrate the Tottenham Hotspurs' historic FA cup Football victory.

It was initially a children's cake - but all can enjoy!

I have substituted raspberries instead of mulberries as the latter are very difficult to find, but if you have them, then do use them.

INGREDIENTS

Serves 16

- 1 cup or 2 sticks (225g) soft unsalted butter

- 1¼ cups (225g) superfine (caster) sugar

- 4 medium eggs, beaten

- 1 tsp. vanilla extract

- 2½ cups (300g) self-rising (self-raising) flour

- 2 tsp. baking powder

- 3 tbsp. milk (as required)

- 12 x 9 inches (30 cm x 23 cm) cake pan

Topping:

- 1 cup (120g) raspberries or mulberries

- 2 tbsp. water

- 1½ cups (300g) powdered (icing) sugar

- 2 tbsp. desiccated coconut (optional)

METHOD

1. Preheat the oven to 350°F (180°C).

2. Prepare the cake pan by greasing and sprinkling a little flour to stop the cake from sticking.

3. Mix the butter and sugar and beat until the mixture turns a lighter color.

4. Beat in the eggs and vanilla extract.

5. Fold in the flour and baking powder.

6. Add milk as required to form a dropping consistency.

7. Pour into the prepared cake pan.

8. Bake for 30-35 minutes, until golden and risen.

9. Leave to cool for a few minutes before turning out onto a cooling rack before icing.

For the topping:

1. Place the raspberries and 2 tablespoons of water in a small saucepan over medium heat and cook for about 5 minutes or until the raspberries start to break down and become jelly-like.

2. Use the back of a spoon to gently press the raspberries through a sieve, catching the precious juices in a small bowl – you should get about 4 tablespoons of juice. If you don't, top up with a splash of water. Discard the raspberry seeds.

3. Add the powdered (icing) sugar to the raspberry juice until you have a thick, smooth icing. Spoon over the cake and smooth using a palette knife. Scatter with the coconut, if using, and leave to set.

4. Once set, slice into squares and share!

Grated coconut was always sprinkled over the icing but invariably caused problems for most Quakers with false teeth, as the coconut would get stuck!

Thank you for joining me on our journey around England. I have had to be very selective about the recipes I've included, as there are many more I could share.

I hope you feel inspired to bake these wonderful treats and that you will enjoy them again and again!

APPENDIX – PASTRY TIPS

INTRODUCTION

Don't let requiring a pastry base put you off! If you don't fancy making your pastry, you don't have to! There are some terrific ready-made pastries available and even ready-cooked pastry shells.

Ready-Made Pastry - be guilt-free!

I like to think of it as having my own sous-chef giving me a helping hand! And what great chef doesn't have a sous-chef to help with the more basic and time-consuming tasks?

You have two options, either buy the tart shells ready-baked and good to go, or buy a ready-made pastry, either in a block or ready-rolled and use that to line your tarts. Let's look at both options.

Ready-baked pastry cases

All you do is to make one of the fillings yourself. Using a ready-baked pastry shell is such a quick way to produce a delicious tart.

I encourage you to try to buy pastry cases that are made with butter as the flavor will be much better. You can buy the small tartlet shells or the larger tarts.

Ready-made pastry, either in a block or ready-rolled

If you fancy being a little more hands-on with the pastry, you can buy a block of ready-made pastry or a pack of ready-rolled pastry. The advantage is that it is already rested and will not shrink when you cook it.

Puff pastry, however, takes much longer to make, and I would recommend buying it ready-made. The results with ready-made puff pastry are so good that it doesn't seem worth your time and energy to make it from scratch.

If you are not in a hurry, have a go at making your own pastry. It is straightforward and delicious!

MAKE YOUR OWN PASTRY

There seems to have grown up a great mystery about pastry-making, and it is sometimes perceived as a complicated and challenging art. But, with a few pointers in mind, it doesn't take long and is very straightforward.

It is impressive that you haven't skipped over this section and moved straight back to the recipes!

You can make it by hand or use a food processor. The advantage of the processor is that it keeps all the ingredients cool, but it is easy to over-work the pastry. If you don't mind a bit of extra washing up, then use the food processor. But if you like to get your hands into the mixture - and it is rather therapeutic - then have a go with your fingertips.

Top tips for fantastic pastry every time

1. Keep everything cool - including yourself!

2. Always rub in the fat into the flour before adding any other ingredients.

3. Make sure the fat is well rubbed in - like breadcrumbs.

4. Only add cold liquids.

5. Allow the pastry to rest before using it for at least 30 minutes.

6. Always use a preheated oven.

7. Always place your cake pan onto a preheated baking sheet as this will keep the bottom crisp as no one likes a soggy bottom!

Shortcrust Pastry

You need all-purpose (plain) flour, butter, salt, and cold water. The usual adage is "half fat to flour," but that is by weight, so only works if you are working in grams. If you are using cup measurements, I have set out the volumes you need.

Shortcrust pastry can be used for everything, but if you like your pastry a little sweeter, I have set out a sweet pastry recipe as well.

Ingredients - This makes 12 oz. (375g) shortcrust pastry enough to line a 9 inch (23 cm) removable bottom cake pan.

- 2 cups (250g) all-purpose (plain) flour

- ½ cup (125g) butter

- 1 tsp. salt

- 2-3 tbsp. cold water as needed

Ingredients - This makes 18 oz. (500g) shortcrust pastry enough to line a 9 inch (23 cm) removable bottom cake pan and make the lid.

- 3 cups (375g) all-purpose (plain) flour

- ¾ cup (170g) butter

- 1½ tsp. salt

- 3-4 tbsp. cold water as needed

Method

Keep yourself and everything cool!

1. Put the flour into a bowl.

2. Add the teaspoon of salt.

3. Cut up the fat into about 1 cm cubes and coat the cubes with flour.

4. With your cool hands, rub-in the fat into the flour by lifting your hands above the bowl, which will aerate the mixture. Or if you are using a processor, gently pulse.

5. When it resembles breadcrumbs, your rubbing-in work is done.

6. Add just enough cold water, so the dough comes together into a firm ball.

7. Press the dough into a disc, sprinkle with a little flour, wrap it in cling film and pop it in the fridge for at least 30 minutes to chill.

RECIPE FOR SHORTCRUST SWEET PASTRY

INGREDIENTS

This makes 14 oz. (425g) sweet shortcrust pastry, generous enough to line a 9 inch (23 cm) removable bottom cake pan.

- 2 cups (250g) all-purpose (plain) flour

- ½ cup (125g) butter

- ¼ cup (50g) superfine (caster) sugar

- 1 large egg

- 2 tbsp. cold milk as needed

METHOD

Keep yourself and everything cool!

1. Put the flour into a bowl.

2. Cut up the fat into about 1 cm cubes and coat the cubes with flour.

3. With your cool hands, rub-in the fat into the flour by lifting your hands above the bowl, which will aerate the mixture. Or if you are using a processor, gently pulse.

4. When it resembles breadcrumbs, your rubbing-in work is done.

5. Add the sugar.

6. Add the egg and enough cold milk so that the dough comes together into a firm ball.

7. Press the dough into a disc, sprinkle with a little flour, wrap it in cling film and pop it in the fridge for at least 30 minutes to chill.

HOW TO ROLL PASTRY

Whether you have made your own pastry or bought a ready-made block, this section is for you. If you are using ready-rolled pastry, then move onto the section below, "How to Bake Blind".

1. Make a disc out of your pastry, sprinkle your cool surface with flour and place your pastry disc on top.

2. Take your rolling pin, and make indents in one direction, turn the pastry and do the same at right angles to the original indents. This will mean that the disc is about twice its original size.

3. Roll out the pastry from the middle away from you, in three short bursts. Turn the pastry 90 degrees and repeat until the dough is the right size for your cake pan.

HOW TO LINE YOUR CAKE PAN

Once you have rolled out your pastry or unrolled your ready-rolled pastry, it is time to line your cake pan.

I think it is best to use a metal pan with a removable bottom so that the tart will come out much easier. If you are using a non-stick pan, then please grease it before sprinkling it with a little flour. There is nothing more upsetting than being unable to get your beautiful creation out of its pan!

1. Ensure the pastry is the right size by carefully placing the cake pan on top of your rolled-out pastry and judging whether there is enough pastry to go up the sides.

2. Take your rolling pin and place the pastry half over the rolling pin and move it over your cake pan.

3. Gently drop the pastry over your tin. Lift the edges to allow the pastry to fall into the edges of the tin.

4. Be careful not to pull or stretch your pastry at this point; just allow it to fall.

5. Gently press it into the corners of the tin.

6. Take your rolling pin and roll over the top of the cake pan. This will sever the excess pastry from your lined tin.

7. Slightly loosen the edges of the pastry with your fingers so that the top is not stuck to the rim.

HOW TO BAKE BLIND

Once you have rolled out your pastry and lined your cake pan, some recipes call for the pastry to be cooked before adding the filling. This is so that the pastry is not soggy on the bottom and is nice and crispy.

1. Preheat the oven to 400°F (200°C).

2. Take some greaseproof paper, parchment paper, or lightly greased aluminum foil and place it over your pastry-lined cake pan.

3. Fill it with something that will weigh down the paper or foil, such as dried beans, or blind baking ceramic balls. Cover the base. Protect the top by ensuring the paper overlaps it so that the edges do not over-brown.

4. Place in the hot oven for 10-15 minutes.

5. Remove the paper carefully with the beans or ceramic balls and pop the cake pan back in the oven for another 10 minutes to cook the base.

6. Take out of the oven and allow to cool.

7. Your tart base is now ready to be filled!

RELEASING YOUR TART FROM THE PAN

An easy way of doing this is to stand the removable bottom cake pan on a can of beans and gently pull down the outer case, releasing your tart.

ARE ALL THESE RULES REALLY NECESSARY?

Coming from a chemistry background, I always like to know the reasons for following the exact instructions in a recipe and whether there are any corners that can successfully be cut. So, I thought it might be helpful for some explanation as to why these guidelines are suggested, and then you can make up your own mind as to whether it is worthwhile. I have suggested the following:

1. **Rest your pastry for at least 30 minutes.** If you don't, it is much softer and more difficult to handle and very likely to shrink away from the cake pan.

2. **Keep everything cold.** If the dough gets too warm, it is much more difficult to handle, and the pastry will be tougher.

3. **Add just enough water to form the dough.** If too little water is added, the pastry will be very dry and break when you try to roll it out (just add a little more water). If too much, it will be too sticky to handle (just add a little more flour).

4. **Do not overwork your pastry.** If you do, the pastry will be rather tough, which is why you need to be careful if you use a food processor.

But most importantly - enjoy and get baking!

ABOUT THE AUTHOR

Sandra Hawkins is qualified in many disciplines. She is a chemist, banker, lawyer, teacher, apologist, author, wife, mother of three and a qualified Indian head massage therapist! However, she also has a real passion for food and is an exceptional chef.

Combining her love for mixing things up in a chemistry lab with her natural gift as a supertaster, Sandra has always loved to experiment with cooking.

From her very first Food and Nutrition lessons at an English school (Guildford High) to exploring Indian and African cuisine while traveling and living overseas, Sandra is particularly passionate about using cooking to bring people together and to seize life's delights and transform them into moments.

This book reflects her passion for food and her unique ability to simplify complex recipes, so people can easily enjoy traditional English teatime treats at home for the first time.

Sandra is married to songwriter/producer/author, Simon Hawkins and has three beautiful children, Poppy, Monty and Barty . They live in a quiet village on a beach on the south coast of England, in West Sussex.

ACKNOWLEDGEMENTS

This book would not have been written without the constant support from my husband, Simon, and my three children, Poppy, Monty and Barty.

A big thank you to my editor, William Gaskill and his team at Precision Content, for making this book what it is.

CPSIA information can be obtained
at www.ICGtesting.com
Printed in the USA
BVHW010943140323
660409BV00017B/281